Animals Are Amazing:

Fun Facts for Kids

written by J.R. Ellis

Animals Are Amazing

Animals come in all shapes and sizes—from tiny insects to massive whales—each with amazing abilities that help them survive.

Some creatures rely on camouflage or dazzling patterns and colors to stay hidden or warn predators. Others have tough defenses like armor, spikes, or venomous weapons to protect themselves. Some animals even have superpowers, like night vision or echolocation, that help them navigate their world. Many species have incredible tails that help them balance, defend, or communicate. Finding food can be a challenge, but clever animals use problem-solving skills and teamwork to hunt or forage successfully. Whether playing, working together, or living in groups, animals develop important skills that keep them strong and safe.

By learning how animals adapt, survive, and thrive, we can better understand and protect the amazing creatures that share our planet.

Did you know?

Orcas, also known as killer whales, are incredibly smart and powerful marine mammals. They live in tight family groups called pods and use complex vocalizations to communicate and coordinate hunting. Orcas are apex predators, meaning nothing hunts them—not even sharks! Some pods specialize in hunting fish, while others work together to tip icebergs and catch seals. Their black-and-white coloring helps them blend into the ocean from above and below, making them excellent ambush hunters with teamwork and strategy on their side.

Did you know?

Horses have been close companions to humans for thousands of years, known for their strength, speed, and loyalty. They can sleep both lying down and standing up, thanks to a special locking system in their legs. Horses use their ears, eyes, and even nostrils to express emotion, and they often form strong bonds with each other—and with people. Each horse has a unique whinny and scent, which helps them recognize friends. They're also excellent at remembering places and people!

Animal Camouflage

Camouflage is like nature's magic trick that helps animals hide and blend into their surroundings! Some animals change their color or pattern to match their environment, making them hard to see. Camouflage helps animals stay safe from predators or sneak up on their food. It can work in different ways: matching the background around them, using patterns to break up their outline, copying the texture or shape around them, or even pretending to be something entirely different. It's an amazing survival trick that can help animals stay hidden or help them find their next meal!

Praying Mantis

The *praying mantis* is a master of disguise, blending into its surroundings by looking like leaves, sticks, or even flowers. This clever camouflage helps it stay hidden from predators and makes it easier to ambush unsuspecting insects. With its stealthy skills, the mantis patiently waits for the perfect moment to strike!

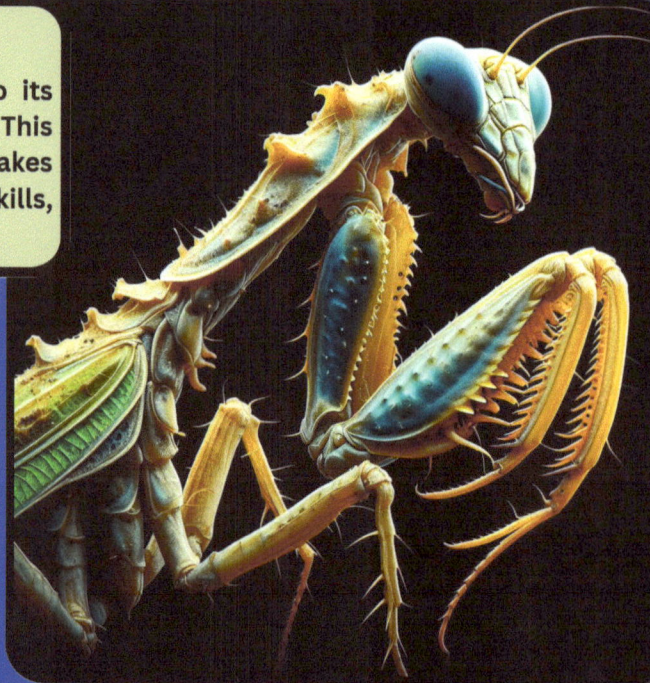

Snowshoe Hare

Snowshoe hares have a built-in seasonal disguise! Their fur changes color to help them blend into their surroundings— turning white in the winter to match the snow and brown in the summer to blend with dirt and plants. This clever camouflage helps them stay hidden from hungry predators all year long!

Tiger

Tigers have a striking orange coat with black stripes that might seem bold, but it actually helps them blend into their surroundings. The tall grasses, dappled sunlight, and deep shadows of the jungle create the perfect background for their camouflage. This stealthy disguise makes it easier for tigers to sneak up on prey, staying hidden until the perfect moment to pounce!

Chameleon

Chameleons can change the color of their skin to blend in with their surroundings, helping them hide from predators and sneak up on prey. But color changes aren't just for camouflage—they also use them to communicate, show emotions, or regulate their body temperature.

Zebra

Zebras may stand out to humans, but their black and white stripes are perfect for blending into the tall grasses of the African plains. Since lions are colorblind, the stripes act as a visual trick, breaking up a zebra's shape. When zebras stand together in a herd, their patterns blend, confusing predators and making it hard to focus on just one zebra to chase!

Patterns and Colors

Animals come in all sorts of patterns and colors, and they aren't just for looking cool! Some animals blend in with their surroundings making them hard to see. Some animals use bright colors to warn others that they might be dangerous or poisonous, while others have awesome colors or patterns to help them attract a mate. In the wild, colors and patterns are nature's amazing way of helping animals communicate, protect themselves and find their friends!

Mandrill

Mandrills have bright blue and red faces that make them one of the most colorful primates. These bold colors aren't just for show—they help mandrills communicate! When a mandrill is excited or feels threatened, its colors become even brighter, sending clear signals to others in the group about its emotions.

Peacock

Peacocks have long, dazzling feathers in shades of blue and green, decorated with eye-like patterns. Males fan out their shimmering tails in a display to attract females. The bigger and brighter the feathers, the more impressive they look, helping them stand out and win the attention of potential mates!

Flamingo

Flamingos are famous for their bright pink feathers, but they aren't born that way! Their color comes from the shrimp and algae they eat, which contain special pigments. The more they eat, the pinker they get! Their vivid feathers help them stand out in their large flocks, making it easier to find each other. A healthy, well-fed flamingo is often the brightest, which can even help attract a mate!

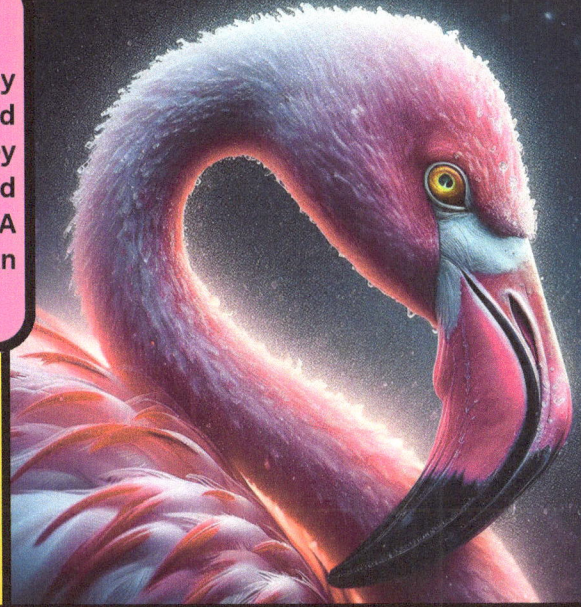

Mantis Shrimp

The *mantis shrimp* boasts a rainbow of colors on its shell, making it one of the most vibrant creatures in the ocean. These bright patterns serve as a warning—this tiny but mighty shrimp can deliver a lightning-fast punch strong enough to crack shells and scare off predators!

Blue Poison Dart Frog

The *blue poison dart frog* may be small, but its bright blue skin sends a powerful message—'Stay away!' Its vivid color warns predators that it is highly toxic. Found in the rainforests of South America, this tiny frog produces poison through its skin, making it dangerous to touch or eat. Predators quickly learn that the brighter the frog, the more dangerous it is, helping the blue poison dart frog stay safe from hungry hunters

Did you know?

The *frill-necked lizard* is famous for the large, colorful frill around its neck, which it flares out when threatened. This sudden display, along with loud hissing, can scare off predators! These lizards can also sprint away on their back legs, looking almost like tiny dinosaurs as they run. Native to Australia and New Guinea, they spend most of their time in trees but quickly drop to the ground when needed. Their dramatic frill isn't just for show—it's an incredible defense mechanism!

Did you know?

Pigs are smarter than many people realize—they can learn tricks, recognize their names, and even play video games with a joystick! With an incredible sense of smell, pigs use their snouts to root through soil and find hidden food. Though they're often associated with mud, pigs only roll in it to stay cool since they don't sweat. Social and curious, pigs form strong bonds with one another and communicate using a variety of grunts and squeals that express everything from excitement to alarm.

Did you know?

Jackrabbits are known for their incredible speed and agility. These long-legged animals can run up to 45 miles per hour and leap over 10 feet in a single bound! Their huge ears help them regulate body temperature in the hot desert sun, acting like natural radiators. Jackrabbits rely on their lightning-quick reflexes and zigzag running to escape predators. During the day, they stay hidden in shallow depressions called "forms," blending into the landscape to avoid being seen.

Did you know?

Llamas are smart, social animals known for their gentle nature and expressive faces. Native to South America, they've been used as pack animals for centuries and can carry up to 25% of their body weight! Llamas hum softly to communicate and can even learn simple commands. When annoyed or threatened, they might spit—usually at each other, not humans! Their thick wool is warm and soft, making it perfect for cold mountain climates.

Animal Defenses

In the wild, animals have some amazing tricks to stay safe from predators! They use clever defenses to protect themselves in all sorts of ways. Some animals have tough shells or hard plates to shield them from harm, while others puff up or change color to look bigger or blend in with their surroundings. Some can even play dead to trick their enemies or roll up into a ball to protect themselves. These amazing defenses help animals stay safe and thrive in their wild homes!

King Cobra

The *king cobra* flattens its neck to create a wide, flared hood when it feels threatened. This dramatic display makes it look bigger and more intimidating to predators. If the warning isn't enough, the cobra can strike with its powerful venomous bite, making it one of the most feared snakes in the world!

Armadillo

Armadillos have tough, bony shells that act like armor, protecting them from predators. When they sense danger, some species can roll into a tight ball, making it nearly impossible for predators to bite or scratch them. Their natural defense helps keep them safe in the wild!

Opossum

The *opossum* has a unique and funny way to avoid danger—it plays dead! When a predator gets too close, the opossum flops over, becomes completely still, and even lets its tongue hang out to look lifeless. It can stay this way for minutes or even hours! Many predators prefer live prey, so when they think the opossum is already dead, they often lose interest and move on, leaving it unharmed.

Turtle

Turtles have hard shells that act like built-in armor, keeping them safe from predators. When they feel threatened, they tuck their heads, legs, and tails inside, making it nearly impossible for most predators to reach them. Their tough shells provide excellent protection in the wild!

Skunk

Skunks have a powerful defense—they spray a stinky liquid when they feel threatened! The foul smell is so strong that it makes predators run away and can linger for days. But skunks don't spray right away! First, they give a warning by stomping their feet, hissing, or raising their tails. If the predator doesn't back off, the skunk lets loose its smelly spray, which can reach up to 10 feet!

Animal Weapons

Animals have some amazing built-in weapons that help them hunt or stay safe! Sharp teeth, talons, and claws are perfect for catching food, while horns and antlers are great for battles with other animals. Some creatures use stingers to defend themselves when danger is near, and others have powerful pincers for protection and moving things. These special tools are crucial for animals to survive in the wild, helping them stay prepared for whatever comes their way!

Eagle

Eagles have powerful, razor-sharp talons that help them snatch fish and small animals right out of the water or off the ground. Their strong grip is so powerful that it can carry prey while flying. Eagles also have hooked beaks designed for tearing meat, making them fierce hunters in the sky!

Elk

Male *elk* use their massive antlers to battle rivals during the mating season. They lock antlers and push against each other in fierce contests of strength. The winner earns the right to lead a group of females. Each year, elk shed their antlers and grow new, larger ones for the next season's battles!

African Lion

Lions are powerful hunters that use their sharp teeth and claws to catch and eat their prey. Their strong jaws can crush bones, while their razor-sharp claws help them grip struggling animals. With a mighty swipe of their powerful paws, they can take down large prey like zebras and antelopes. Working together in groups called prides, lions use teamwork and strength to bring down even the biggest animals on the savanna!

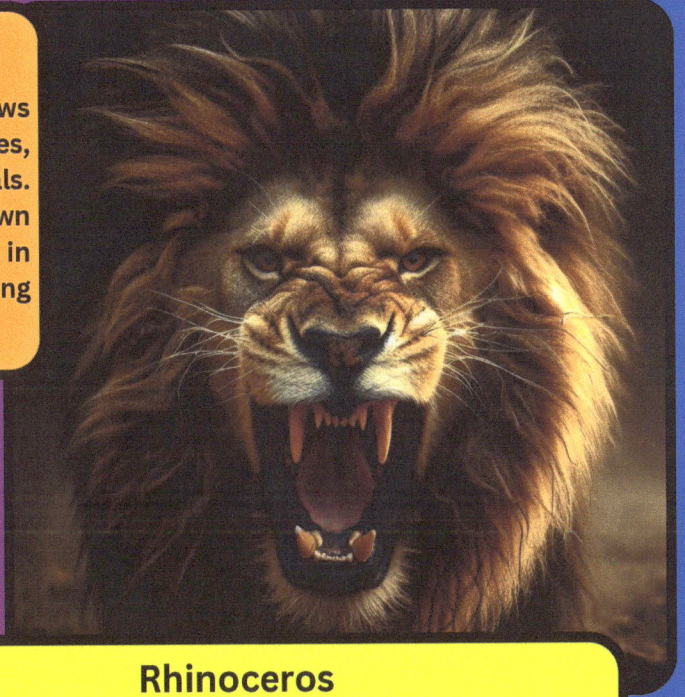

Rhinoceros

Rhinos use their sharp, sturdy horns to protect themselves from predators and rivals. When threatened, they can charge at incredible speeds, using their massive bodies like battering rams. Their horns are made of keratin, the same material as human fingernails, and grow back if damaged!

Alligator

Alligators have incredibly strong jaws filled with sharp teeth that help them grab and hold onto prey. Their powerful bite can crush bones, making escape nearly impossible. Once they have their meal, they use a deadly move called the "death roll" where they spin their bodies in the water to tear prey apart. This powerful attack helps them take down animals like wild boars, deer, and even cattle that wander too close to the water !

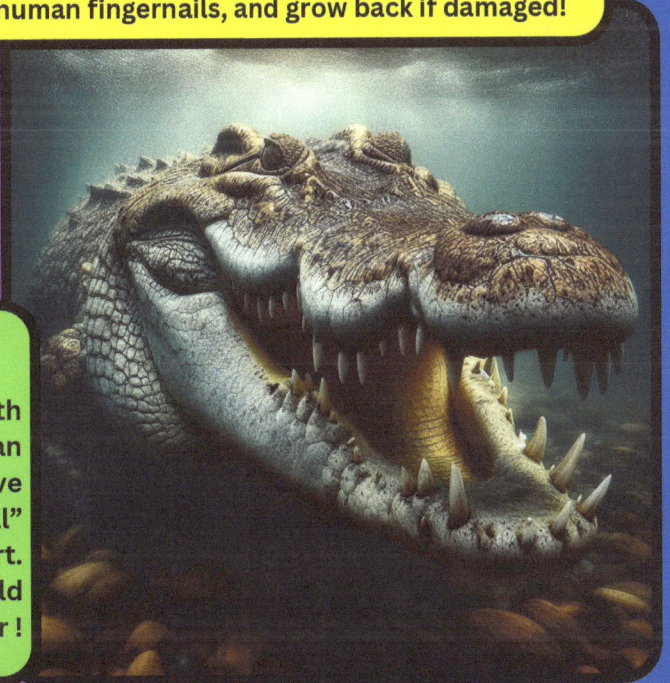

Did you know?

Pangolins are the only mammals completely covered in scales made of keratin—the same protein found in our nails and hair. When threatened, they curl into a tight, armored ball that's nearly impossible for predators to penetrate. These shy, nocturnal creatures use their super-long, sticky tongues—sometimes longer than their body!—to slurp up ants and termites. With strong claws for digging and a keen sense of smell, pangolins are perfectly built for their insect-eating lifestyle.

Did you know?

Walruses are massive marine mammals known for their long tusks, which can grow over three feet long! These tusks help them pull their heavy bodies out of the water and show dominance within their herd. Walruses use their super-sensitive whiskers to detect shellfish on the ocean floor, even in complete darkness. They can slow their heart rate to dive deeper and stay underwater longer. With thick blubber and tough skin, they're built to survive freezing Arctic waters and icy conditions.

Did you know?

Quokkas are small marsupials from Australia often called "the world's happiest animals" because of their constant smile-like expressions. But they're more than just cute faces! Quokkas can survive on very little water and even go months without drinking by getting moisture from leaves. They are mainly nocturnal and hop like tiny kangaroos. When threatened, a mother quokka may drop her joey to distract predators while she escapes—a harsh but effective survival trick.

Did you know?

Bighorn sheep are famous for their massive, curled horns and incredible mountain-climbing skills. Males, called rams, use their horns to clash in headbutting battles that can last for hours! These powerful rams can charge each other at speeds over 20 miles per hour, and their thick skulls help absorb the impact. Bighorn sheep live on rocky cliffs and steep slopes, where their split hooves and strong legs give them excellent balance. Their sharp vision helps them spot predators from far away.

Animal Superpowers

While humans use five senses—sight, hearing, smell, taste, and touch—some animals have super special senses that help them explore the world in amazing ways. Some can use sound waves to see in the dark, while others sense tiny electric signals from far away. There are animals that detect vibrations in the ground or use their sense of smell to find food from miles away. These unique skills let animals sense things beyond what humans can see or hear, making them fantastic at surviving and thriving in their environments.

Great White Shark

Great white sharks have special sensors that detect tiny electrical signals from other animals in the water. This ability helps them find prey even in murky waters or complete darkness. With this built-in radar, they can sense movement, locate hiding fish, and strike with incredible accuracy!

Pigeon

Pigeons have an incredible sense of direction, allowing them to find their way home from miles away. They use Earth's magnetic field like a built-in compass, helping them navigate even when landmarks aren't visible. This amazing skill makes them some of the best navigators in the animal kingdom!

Copperhead

Snakes have a superpower—they use their tongues to 'smell' the air! The *Copperhead*, a type of pit viper, flicks its tongue to collect scent particles and brings them to a special organ in its mouth called the Jacobson's organ. In addition to this keen sense, Copperheads have heat-sensing pit organs that help them detect warm-blooded prey, even in the dark. By combining these abilities, they become stealthy hunters, striking with precision when prey comes close.

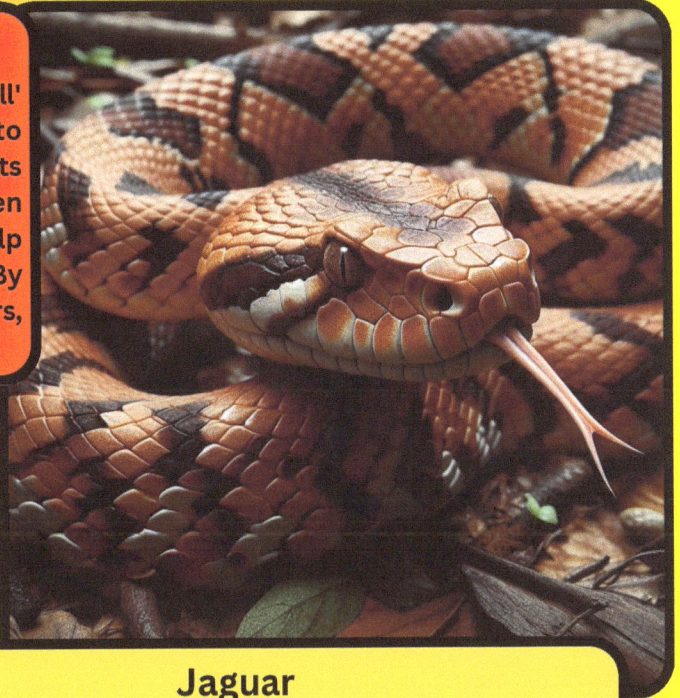

Jaguar

Jaguars have incredible night vision, allowing them to see and hunt in near darkness. Their eyes are six times more sensitive to light than human eyes, helping them spot prey in dense jungles at night. This super sight makes them top nocturnal predators!

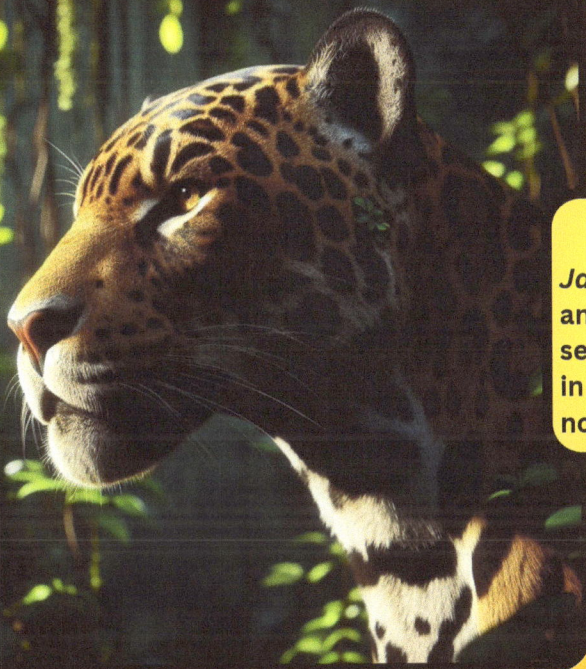

Electric Eel

Electric eels have an amazing ability—they generate electric fields to sense their surroundings and locate prey, even in the darkest, murkiest waters. These electric pulses act like a built-in radar, helping them navigate and detect movement nearby. When hunting, they release powerful shocks of up to 600 volts to stun fish and other prey, making them one of the most electrifying predators in the animal kingdom!

Amazing Tails

Tails are like nature's super-tools, and they come in all shapes and sizes! Animals use their tails for all sorts of amazing things. Some tails help with balance when animals hop or climb, while others are perfect for swimming or sending messages to friends. Some tails swat away pests, like flies, and some can even grab things like an extra hand. Tails can also be used as tools or weapons to help animals do awesome things in their wild homes.

Arctic Fox

Arctic foxes have thick, bushy tails that act like built-in blankets in freezing temperatures. When they sleep, they curl into a tight ball and wrap their fluffy tails around their faces to stay warm. Their dense fur and insulated tails help them survive the harsh, icy Arctic winters!

Beaver

Beavers have flat, paddle-like tails that help them swim swiftly through the water. Their tails also act as a warning system—when danger is near, they slap the water with a loud 'smack' to alert other beavers. In winter, their tails store fat to help them survive the cold months!

Eastern Diamondback Rattlesnake

The *Eastern Diamondback Rattlesnake* has a built-in warning system—its rattle! When threatened, it vibrates the end of its tail, creating a loud buzzing sound to scare off predators. This warning helps avoid unnecessary fights, since the Eastern Diamondback prefers to be left alone. The rattle is made of hollow segments that click together when shaken. The more a rattlesnake sheds its skin, the more segments it adds, making its warning even louder!

Scorpion

Scorpions have powerful, curved tails tipped with a venomous stinger, which they use for both hunting and defense. When threatened, they arch their tails over their bodies, ready to strike in an instant. Their venom helps them paralyze prey, making it easier to catch and eat.

Spider Monkey

Spider monkeys have long, prehensile tails that act like an extra hand! They use their tails to grip branches, hang upside down, and even grab food. Their strong tails help them swing swiftly through the treetops, making them expert climbers in the rainforest canopy. These tails are so powerful that spider monkeys can dangle by them while using all four limbs to eat, groom, or interact with other monkeys in their group!

Did you know?

Yaks are shaggy, mountain-dwelling animals built to survive some of the coldest climates on Earth. Their thick woolly coats and large lungs help them stay warm and breathe in the thin air of high altitudes. Yaks can climb steep mountain paths and carry heavy loads for long distances. They're also surprisingly agile for their size! In the wild, yaks live in herds and graze on tough grasses, while domesticated yaks are vital to mountain communities for their milk, meat, and wool.

Did you know?

The *fossa* (pronounced FOO-sah) is a mysterious predator found only on the island of Madagascar. Though it looks like a mix between a cat and a mongoose, the fossa is actually in its own unique family. Agile and sleek, it can climb trees as easily as it runs on the ground. Fossas are top predators in Madagascar, hunting lemurs and other small animals. With sharp claws, powerful jaws, and long tails for balance, the fossa is one of the island's most fascinating and elusive hunters.

Did you know?

Narwhals are known as the "unicorns of the sea" thanks to the long, spiral tusk that males grow from a tooth! This tusk can reach up to 10 feet long and may be used to sense the environment, attract mates, or show dominance. Narwhals live in Arctic waters and dive to incredible depths—over a mile beneath the surface—to hunt for squid, fish, and shrimp. Despite their magical appearance, narwhals are real and specially adapted for life in cold, icy oceans.

Did you know?

The *Indian star tortoise* gets its name from the bright, star-like patterns on its shell, which help it blend into dry grasses and leaf litter. This clever camouflage protects it from predators. Native to India and Sri Lanka, this tortoise prefers dry forests and scrublands. Unlike many reptiles, it's mostly herbivorous, munching on leaves, fruits, and flowers. Its domed shell isn't just beautiful—it also helps the tortoise roll upright if it gets flipped over!

Hunting and Finding Food

Animals have many clever ways to find food, each suited to their needs. Some are expert hunters that chase and catch prey, while others forage for plants or insects. Animals use different tools and techniques to get their meals. Whether they are hunting, gathering, or scavenging, each animal has developed its own special strategy to find the food it needs to stay healthy and strong. Some even use teamwork to hunt larger prey. Finding food is a crucial part of survival, and animals have amazing skills to help them do just that.

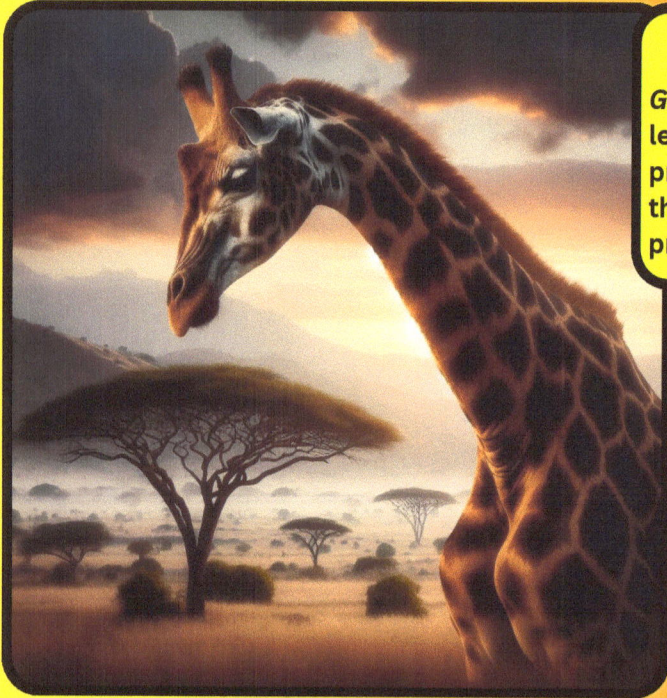

Giraffe

Giraffes have incredibly long necks that help them reach leaves high up in trees, where other animals can't reach. Their prehensile tongues, which can grow up to 18 inches long, help them grab food with ease. Their height also allows them to spot predators from far away, allowing them to escape danger.

Komodo Dragon

Komodo dragons are patient and stealthy hunters, using ambush tactics to surprise their prey. With a powerful bite, they inject venom that weakens their target and preventing clotting. Instead of chasing, they follow their prey for miles, waiting for it to collapse before moving in to feast.

Black Bear

Black bears are excellent foragers with an incredible sense of smell, allowing them to detect food from miles away. In the months leading up to hibernation, they eat as much as possible, consuming berries, nuts, fish, and even insects to build up fat reserves. Their powerful claws help them dig up roots, tear apart logs for insects, and raid beehives for honey and larvae. They are also skilled climbers, often scaling trees to escape danger, search for food, or find a safe place to rest.

Giant Anteater

Giant anteaters are the largest of the four anteater species and can eat over 30,000 ants and termites in a single day! Instead of teeth, they have an incredibly long, sticky tongue that flicks in and out up to 150 times per minute to scoop up their tiny prey.

Nile Crocodile

Nile crocodiles are expert ambush predators, silently stalking their prey from beneath the water's surface. They wait near the water's edge, striking with lightning speed when animals come to drink or bathe. Their powerful jaws clamp down with incredible force, preventing escape. Once caught, the crocodile drags its prey underwater to drown it before using a brutal 'death roll' to tear it apart. These stealthy hunters can take down zebras, wildebeests, and even humans.

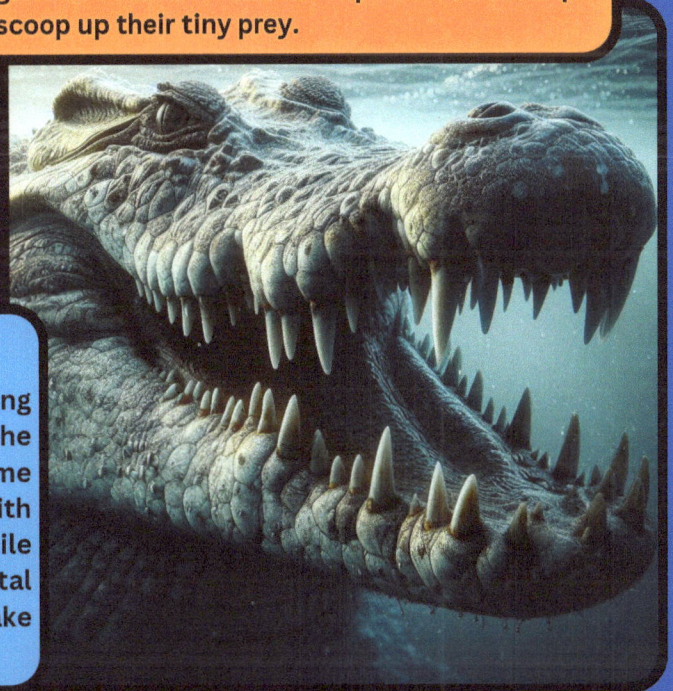

Problem-Solving Skills

Did you know that some animals are amazing problem-solvers, using their smarts and creativity to survive in the wild? Many clever animals have learned to use tools, like sticks or rocks, to help them find food, build homes, or defend themselves. But it doesn't stop there—some animals show amazing problem-solving skills in other ways! They solve puzzles, work together in teams, or come up with clever tricks to outsmart predators or catch their next meal. Whether it's using objects to get what they need or finding creative solutions to challenges, these smart creatures show that animals can be very resourceful.

Koala

Koalas solve the problem of conserving energy by sleeping up to 20 hours a day! Their long naps help them digest eucalyptus leaves, which are low in nutrients but their main food source. With specialized stomachs to break down toxins in the leaves, koalas stay safe while munching on their favorite meal.

Sea Otter

Besides being super cute, *sea otters* are also one of the few animals that use tools! They float on their backs and place a rock on their bellies, smashing clams and sea urchins against it to crack them open. Their thick fur keeps them warm in cold waters, making them well-adapted marine mammals.

Chimpanzee

Chimpanzees are highly intelligent and resourceful, using tools to solve problems and find food. They use sticks to dig into termite mounds, pulling them out covered in insects for a tasty snack. They've also been observed using leaves and moss to soak up water like a sponge for drinking. Some even crack open nuts with rocks, showing incredible problem-solving skills. These behaviors make chimpanzees one of the most skilled tool-users in the animal kingdom!

Rat

Rats are excellent problem-solvers, quickly learning to navigate mazes and puzzles to find food. They adapt to new situations, remember paths, and even work together to succeed. Their intelligence and ability to learn from past experiences helps them thrive in complex environments!

Egyptian Vulture

Egyptian vultures are clever problem-solvers that use tools to access food. When they come across tough eggs, like ostrich eggs, they pick up small rocks in their beaks and drop them onto the shell until it cracks open. This smart technique allows them to reach the nutritious meal inside. Their ability to use tools makes them one of the most intelligent birds of prey, proving that vultures are more than just scavengers!

Did you know?

Weasels may be small, but they're fierce and fast! These sleek hunters have long, flexible bodies that allow them to chase prey through tight burrows and narrow spaces. Don't let their size fool you—they can take down animals much larger than themselves. In colder regions, some weasels turn white in winter to blend in with the snow. They're also known for their "war dance," a wild, bouncy display that confuses prey and makes hunting easier.

Did you know?

Manatees, often called "sea cows," are gentle giants that glide through warm coastal waters and rivers. Despite their size, they're herbivores, munching on seagrass and aquatic plants for up to eight hours a day! Manatees can hold their breath for up to 20 minutes when resting, though they usually surface every few minutes. These peaceful creatures have no natural predators, but they're often injured by boat propellers. Fun fact: their closest land relatives are elephants!

Did you know?

The *duck-billed platypus* is one of the most unusual animals on Earth! It lays eggs, has a bill like a duck, a tail like a beaver, and webbed feet. Found only in Australia, it uses electroreception in its bill to detect tiny movements and electric signals from prey underwater. Males even have venomous spurs on their hind legs. Though it looks like a mix of animals, the platypus is a real mammal—one of only a few that lays eggs!

Did you know?

Lobsters may look ancient—and they are! These fascinating crustaceans have blue blood, due to the copper in their system, and can regenerate lost claws, legs, and antennae. They use their strong claws for crushing and cutting food, and can live for decades in the wild. Lobsters also have teeth in their stomachs to help grind up meals! Though often thought to be red, they're usually greenish-brown or blue until cooked. Some rare lobsters are even yellow, white, or bright blue!

Working and Living in Groups

Many animals live and work together in groups to help each other thrive! By teaming up, animals can share tasks, find food more easily, and protect one another from dangers. Some animals form large groups to stay safe from predators, while others work together to build homes or raise their young. Whether they are hunting, gathering food, or keeping warm, working as a team makes these animals stronger and more successful in their environment. Teamwork is an amazing survival strategy that helps animals stay safe and happy!

Penguin

Penguins survive freezing temperatures by huddling together in large groups, creating a living shield against the cold. They take turns standing on the outer edges, and slowly rotate so every penguin gets a chance to stay warm in the center. This teamwork helps them conserve heat and survive harsh winters.

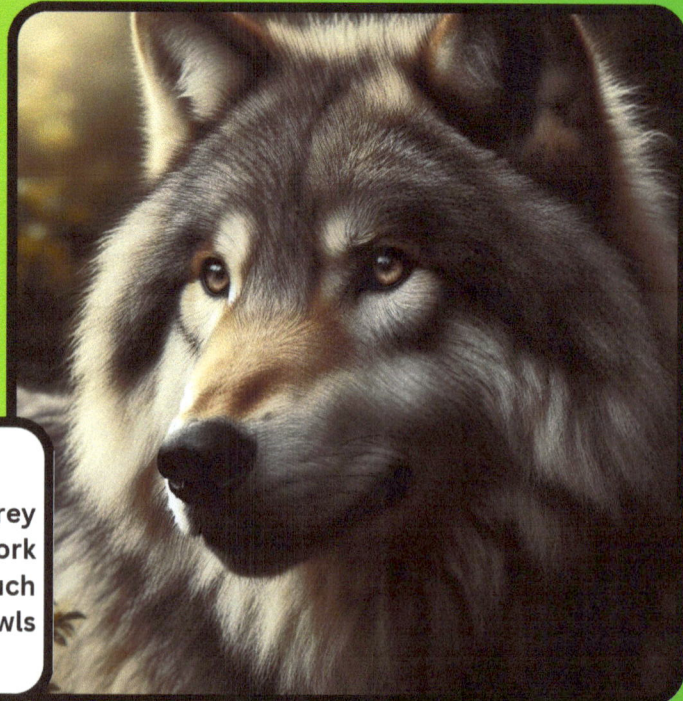

Gray Wolf

Gray wolves live in packs, working together to hunt large prey like deer and elk. They run miles each night, using teamwork and strategy to track, chase, and take down animals much bigger than themselves. Wolves communicate through howls and body language when hunting, playing or raising pups.

Meerkat

Meerkats live in close-knit groups called clans, where teamwork is essential for survival. They take turns standing guard, keeping watch for predators while others search for food. These expert diggers create complex underground tunnels for shelter and protection. Meerkats also help raise each other's pups, teaching them how to find food and stay safe. Their strong family bonds and cooperation make them one of the most social animals in the desert!

Baboon

Baboons live in large troops, where they work together to find food, protect one another, and care for their young. They use loud calls, facial expressions, and body language to communicate, warning the group of danger and keeping their social structure strong.

Macaw

Macaws are intelligent, social birds that thrive in flocks of up to 30 birds, where they work together to find food like nuts, fruits, and seeds. Their strong beaks help them crack open tough shells, and they even share food with their mates. Flying in groups helps them stay safe from predators, and their loud calls allow them to communicate over long distances, keeping their flock connected as they soar through the jungle canopy.

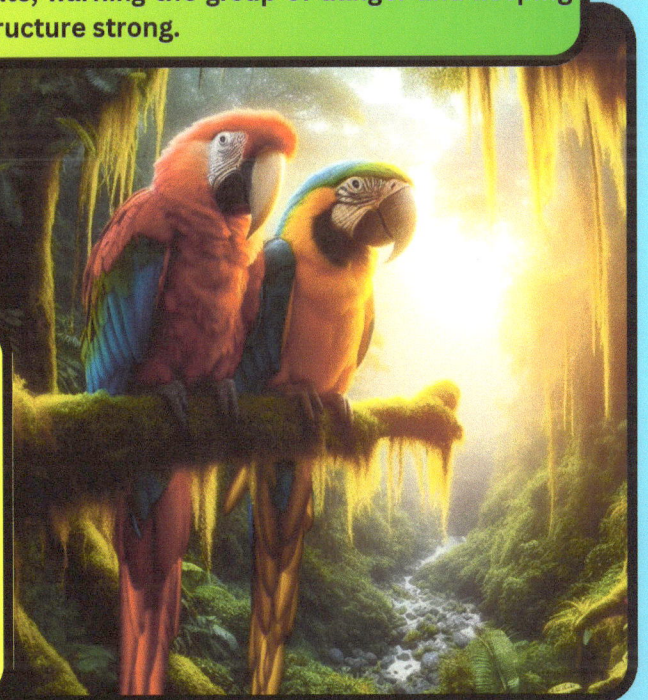

How Animals Play

In the animal world, speed can make a big difference when it comes to survival! Some animals are incredibly fast, allowing them to catch their food or escape from danger. Speedy creatures, like certain fish and birds, can zoom through the water or dive at amazing speeds to find their meals. However, being slow has its advantages too—animals like sloths and tortoises move steadily, conserving energy and blending into their surroundings. Whether they are speedy hunters or slow movers, animals have adapted their speed to fit their lifestyles and needs in the wild.

Lion Cubs

Lion cubs love to pounce, wrestle, and chase each other around the pride. These playful activities help them develop strength, speed, and coordination, sharpening their hunting skills for adulthood. Through play, they also learn social bonds and teamwork, preparing them for life in the pride.

Bear Cubs

Bear cubs love to wrestle, chase, and tumble through the forest, turning play into lessons for the future. These playful battles help them build strength, coordination, and agility. By practicing hunting moves and defensive skills, they prepare for life in the wild, learning how to survive and protect themselves.

Raven

Ravens are incredibly clever birds that love to play in many ways. They slide down snowy hills, play tag and hide-and-seek, and even pull pranks on other animals! These playful activities aren't just for fun—they help ravens sharpen their problem-solving skills, build social bonds, and test their intelligence. Some ravens have even been seen using sticks as toys, showing just how creative and curious these fascinating birds can be!

Goat

Goat kids love to run, jump, and head-butt each other in playful battles. Their energetic games help them build strength, balance, and coordination. By practicing these skills, they learn how to defend themselves and navigate steep, rocky terrain as they grow.

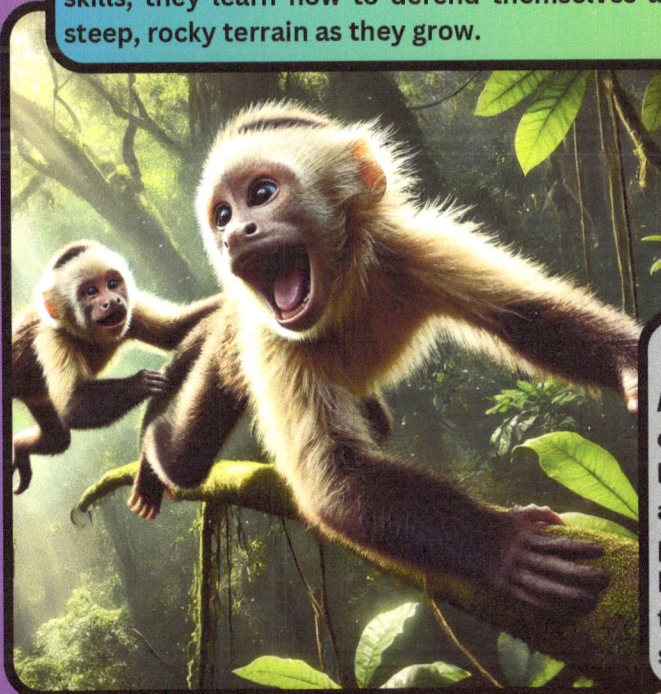

Monkey

Monkeys love to play, spending hours swinging from trees, chasing each other, and wrestling in playful games of tag. They leap, tumble, and dangle by their tails, building strength and agility. Their play isn't just for fun—it helps young monkeys practice climbing, improve coordination, and strengthen social bonds within their troop. By playing together, they learn teamwork, communication, and the skills they all need to survive in the wild.

For Bryce and Jack

ISBN: 978-1-969494-03-1

www.ingramcontent.com/pod-product-compliance
Lightning Source LLC
Chambersburg PA
CBHW060854270326
41934CB00002B/133